Atlas
of
Britain
Picture Book

Stephanie Turnbull

Designed by Doriana Berkovic and Sam Chandler

Illustrated by Colin King

Additional illustrations by
Stuart Trotter and Non Figg

2	Britain and the UK
4	London
6	The West Country
8	The South Coast
10	The Heart of England
12	East Anglia
14	The West Midlands
15	The East Midlands
16	Northwest England
18	Northeast England
20	Wales
22	Southern Scotland
24	Central Scotland
26	Northern Scotland
28	Northern Ireland
30	Index

Britain and the UK

Britain is the largest island in Europe. It is made up of three countries: England, Scotland and Wales. Britain and Northern Ireland are together known as the United Kingdom (UK). The Republic of Ireland and the Isle of Man are not part of the UK.

Shetland Islands

Western Isles

Orkney Islands

NORTH SEA

SCOTLAND

ATLANTIC OCEAN

EDINBURGH

NORTHERN IRELAND

BELFAST

Isle of Man

REPUBLIC OF IRELAND

IRISH SEA

ENGLAND

WALES

CARDIFF

LONDON

This map shows Britain, Northern Ireland and other small islands that are part of the United Kingdom. Each country's capital is marked.

Isles of Scilly

ENGLISH CHANNEL

UK flags

The flags of England, Scotland and Ireland combine to form the flag of the UK. This is called the Union Flag, but is usually known as the Union Jack. Wales had already united with England when the first Union Jack was created, in 1606, so the Welsh flag isn't included in the design. The St. Patrick's Cross was included when Ireland became part of the United Kingdom in 1801, and still represents Northern Ireland.

The Union Flag

St. George's Cross of England

The Red Dragon of Wales

St. Andrew's Cross of Scotland

St. Patrick's Cross of Ireland

People and language

There are over 60 million people living in the UK. The main language is English, although Scotland, Wales and Ireland have their own languages too. Many people from other parts of the world have also settled in Britain.

Governments

The UK is run by an elected government, led by the Prime Minister, and the Queen is the head of state. Wales, Northern Ireland and Scotland also have their own governments, which help to run each country.

This is Saint Edward's Crown, which is worn at the coronation of new kings and queens.

Locator maps

The maps on pages 4–29 each have a small locator map of the UK next to them. The red part tells you which area is shown on the large map.

This locator map goes with the large map of East Anglia.

Usborne Internet Links

For links to websites where you can find out more about Great Britain and Northern Ireland, go to the Usborne Quicklinks website at **www.usborne.com/quicklinks** and type in the keywords '**atlas of Britain picture book**'.

Please read our internet safety guidelines on the Usborne Quicklinks website.

London

London is the capital city of England. Around eight million people live there, making it Europe's largest city. It has all kinds of museums and galleries, as well as many large parks. This map shows the middle of the city, where many museums and shops are found.

Internet links
For links to websites where you can find out more about London, go to
www.usborne.com/quicklinks

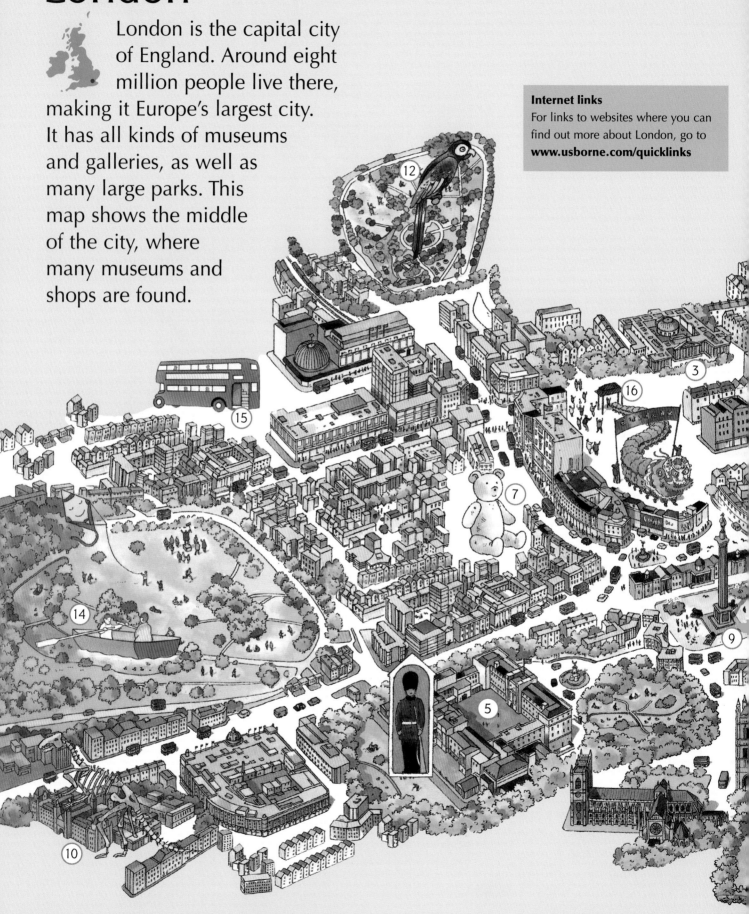

Dinosaur display

The Natural History Museum is one of the largest museums in Europe. It is famous for its spectacular dinosaur exhibits, which include lifelike moving models and a 26m (85ft) long Diplodocus skeleton.

Chinatown

Chinatown is a small part of central London that has become one of the capital's main tourist attractions. Its streets are lined with Chinese restaurants, and every year local Chinese people have a big parade to celebrate Chinese New Year.

Things to spot

1 Tower of London
2 Shakespeare's Globe
3 British Museum
4 Clock tower, Houses of Parliament
5 Guard, Buckingham Palace
6 London Eye
7 Hamleys toy store
8 St. Paul's Cathedral
9 Nelson's Column
10 Dinosaur, Natural History Museum
11 Tower Bridge
12 Parrot, London Zoo
13 HMS Belfast
14 Boating, Hyde Park
15 London bus
16 Chinese New Year parade, Chinatown

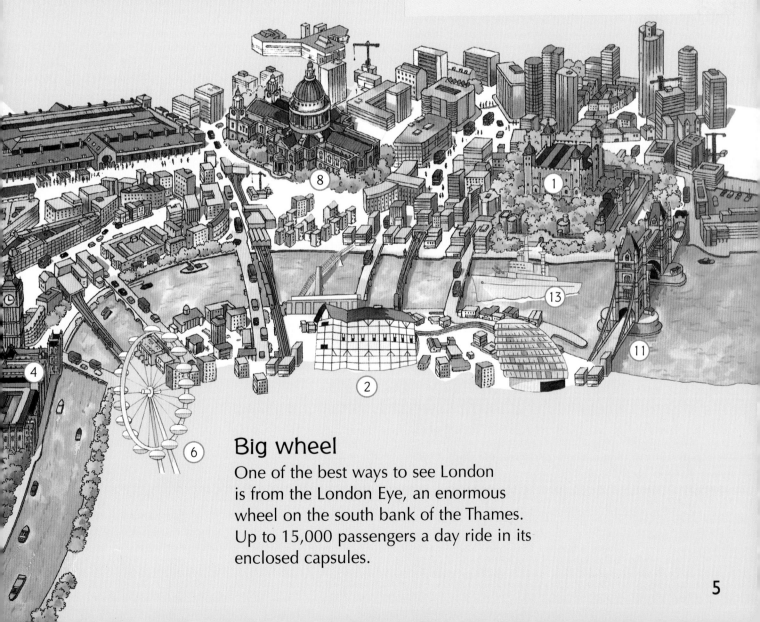

Big wheel

One of the best ways to see London is from the London Eye, an enormous wheel on the south bank of the Thames. Up to 15,000 passengers a day ride in its enclosed capsules.

5

The West Country

The southwestern corner of England is known as the West Country. It has sandy beaches along the coast, and lush fields and high moors further inland. The West Country is often warmer and sunnier than the rest of Britain.

Rocky ruins

Tintagel Castle stands high on a cliff top beside the Atlantic Ocean. The castle was built in the thirteenth century and is now in ruins. Many people believe that King Arthur, a legendary British ruler in ancient times, was born in an older castle on the same spot.

Giant domes

The Eden Project, in Cornwall, consists of two sets of linked domes that form two huge greenhouses. Different climates from around the world are recreated inside the greenhouses, so that thousands of amazing plants are able to grow there.

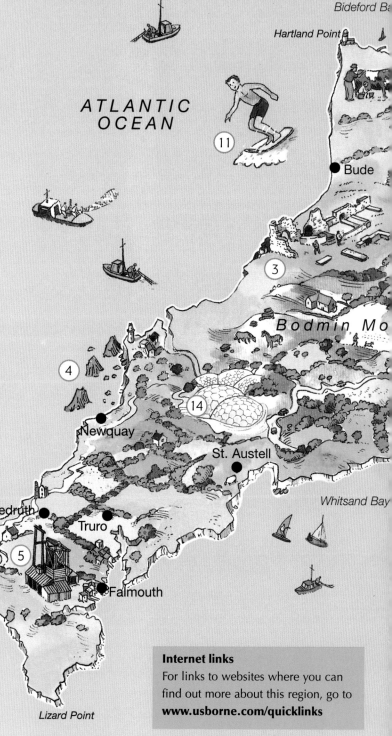

Lundy Island

Barnstaple
Bideford Ba

Hartland Point

ATLANTIC OCEAN

11

Bude

3

Bodmin Mo

4

14

Newquay

St. Austell

Whitsand Bay

Redruth

Truro

5

Falmouth

Penzance

9

Land's End

Mount's Bay

6

Isles of Scilly

Lizard Point

Internet links
For links to websites where you can find out more about this region, go to
www.usborne.com/quicklinks

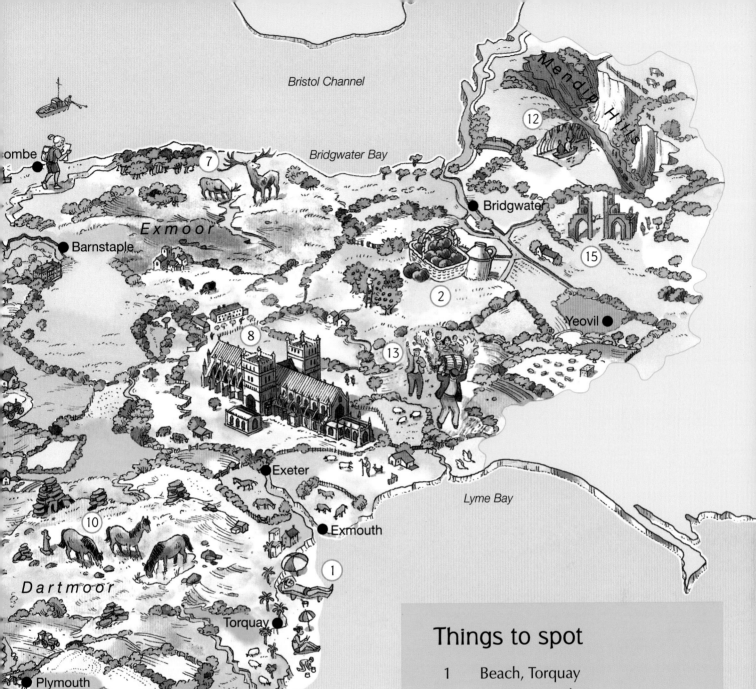

Map labels:
Bristol Channel
Bridgwater Bay
7
Mendip Hills
12
Bridgwater
2
15
Exmoor
Barnstaple
ombe
8
Yeovil
13
Exeter
Lyme Bay
Exmouth
10
1
Dartmoor
Torquay
Plymouth
Start Point

Fiery festival

The town of Ottery St. Mary holds an unusual festival on November 5th each year. Local men run through the streets, carrying barrels of burning tar. When the barrels are too hot to hold, they are rolled along the ground until they fall apart.

Things to spot

1   Beach, Torquay
2   Somerset apples
3   Tintagel Castle
4   Bedruthan Steps
5   Poldark Tin Mine
6   Tropical garden, Tresco
7   Deer, Exmoor National Park
8   Exeter Cathedral
9   St. Michael's Mount
10   Ponies, Dartmoor
11   Surfing, Atlantic Ocean
12   Wookey Hole Caves
13   Ottery St. Mary fire festival
14   Eden Project
15   Glastonbury Abbey

The South Coast

Along England's south coast are many wide beaches, steep white cliffs and popular seaside resorts. Most visitors to Britain arrive at London's airports, the south coast's busy sea ports, or come via the Channel Tunnel rail link.

Yacht races

Every August, hundreds of yachts from all over the world take part in boat races in the sea around the Isle of Wight. The eight-day event is known as Cowes Week.

Andover

Basingstoke

15

Hampshire Downs

Winchester

Cranborne Chase

New Forest

Southampton

1

North Dorset Downs

Portsmouth

9

Bournemouth

Poole

Selsey Bill

6

The Solent

Lyme Bay

South Dorset Downs

Newport

Isle of Wight

12

Chesil Beach

Weymouth

Isle of Portland

The Needles

St. Catherine's Point

Bill of Portland

Cricket champions

In the 1750s, one of England's most famous cricket clubs was formed in the village of Hambledon. The team became very successful and they recorded many of the rules that are still used. The game of cricket might have started as far back as the 1200s.

City by the sea

Brighton is a lively seaside town. It has a long pier, crammed with amusement arcades and souvenir stalls. Another famous landmark is the Royal Pavilion, a huge white building that is designed to look like an Indian palace.

LONDON

Gravesend

North Foreland

Margate

Croydon

11

Canterbury

13

5

Reigate

Maidstone

uildford

North Downs

Ashford

Dover

10

Folkestone

Horsham

Royal Tunbridge Wells

8

14

4

Dungeness

7

ENGLISH CHANNEL

South Downs

Hastings

Worthing Brighton

Eastbourne

Newhaven

Beachy Head

Internet links

For links to websites where you can find out more about this region, go to **www.usborne.com/quicklinks**

Things to spot

1	National Motor Museum, Beaulieu
2	Cricket match, Hambledon
3	Chessington World of Adventures
4	Drusillas Park, Alfriston
5	Dover Castle
6	HMS Victory, Portsmouth
7	Royal Pavilion, Brighton
8	Channel Tunnel
9	Maiden Castle hill fort, Dorchester
10	Gatwick Airport
11	Canterbury Cathedral
12	Yachting, near the Isle of Wight
13	Leeds Castle
14	Bluebell Railway, near East Grinstead
15	Farnborough International air show
16	Olympic Stadium, London

Underwater trains

The Channel Tunnel is the world's longest undersea rail link. It lies under the English Channel and connects Britain and France. Fast passenger trains take just 21 minutes to travel from one end to the other.

The Heart of England

The central part of England contains historic houses and mysterious ancient sites. There is also beautiful countryside, such as the Chilterns, with their rolling chalk hills, and the Cotswolds, which are dotted with pretty villages.

Amazing maze

Longleat House, in Wiltshire, is an Elizabethan mansion that is open to the public. The gardens around it contain a safari park and a massive hedge maze, made up of more than 16,000 yew trees.

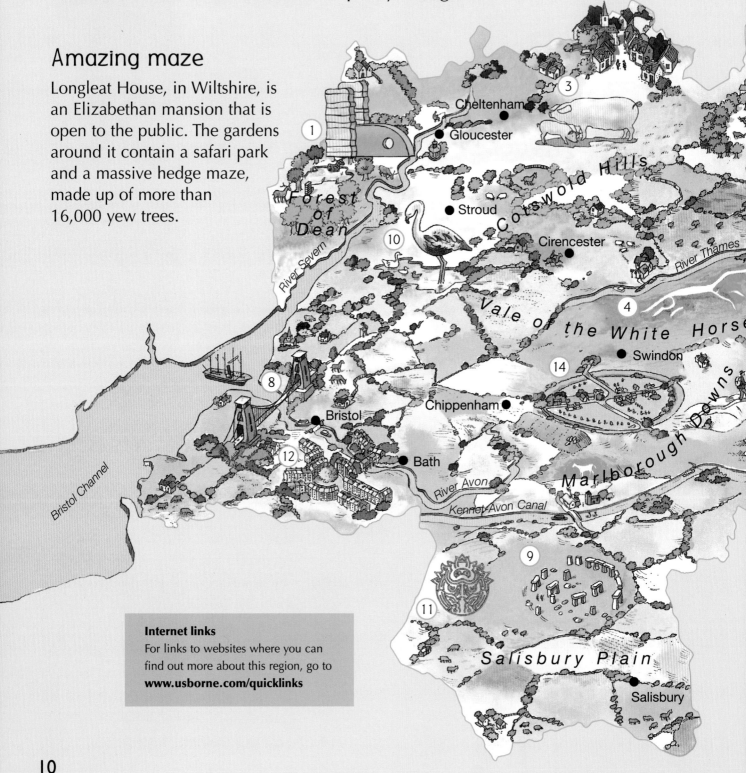

Cheltenham

Gloucester

Forest of Dean

River Severn

Stroud

Cotswold Hills

Cirencester

River Thames

Vale of the White Horse

Swindon

Chippenham

Bristol

Bath

River Avon

Kennet-Avon Canal

Marlborough Downs

Bristol Channel

Salisbury Plain

Salisbury

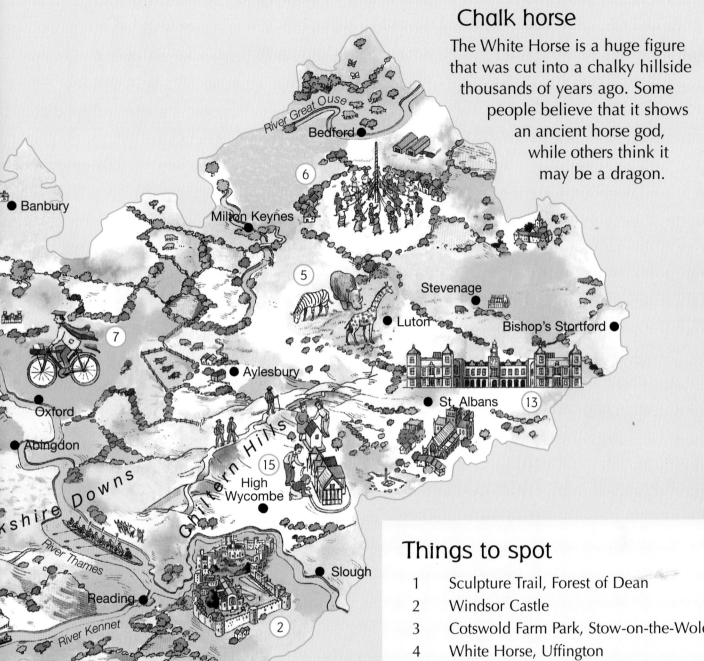

Chalk horse

The White Horse is a huge figure that was cut into a chalky hillside thousands of years ago. Some people believe that it shows an ancient horse god, while others think it may be a dragon.

River Great Ouse

Banbury

Bedford

6

Milton Keynes

5

Stevenage

Luton

Bishop's Stortford

Aylesbury

Oxford

St. Albans

13

Abingdon

Chiltern Hills

15

High Wycombe

Berkshire Downs

River Thames

Slough

Reading

River Kennet

2

Ancient stone circles

More than 5,000 years ago, many rings of stone pillars were constructed in the English countryside. Two of the most spectacular sites are Stonehenge and Avebury, where many of the stones still stand. No one is sure what the circles were for. They may have been ancient temples or burial sites.

Things to spot

1   Sculpture Trail, Forest of Dean
2   Windsor Castle
3   Cotswold Farm Park, Stow-on-the-Wold
4   White Horse, Uffington
5   Whipsnade Wild Animal Park, Dunstable
6   Maypole dancing, Ickwell Green
7   Student, Oxford University
8   Clifton Suspension Bridge, Bristol
9   Stonehenge
10   Wildfowl and Wetlands Centre, Slimbridge
11   Maze, Longleat House, Warminster
12   Georgian houses, Bath
13   Hatfield House
14   Stone circle, Avebury
15   Bekonscot Model Village, Beaconsfield

East Anglia

East Anglia is the round part of eastern England that juts out into the North Sea. It is famous for its flat landscape, known as the Fens. This area was once marshland, but has now been drained, leaving rich soil, which is ideal for growing grain, fruit and vegetables.

NORTH SEA

Norfolk Broads

Great Yarmouth

Lowestoft

River Yare

Norwich

East Dereham

Skegness

Louth

Lincolnshire Wolds

Lincoln

Boston

The Wash

King's Lynn

Wisbech

River Great Ouse

Ely

The Fens

Peterborough

Grantham

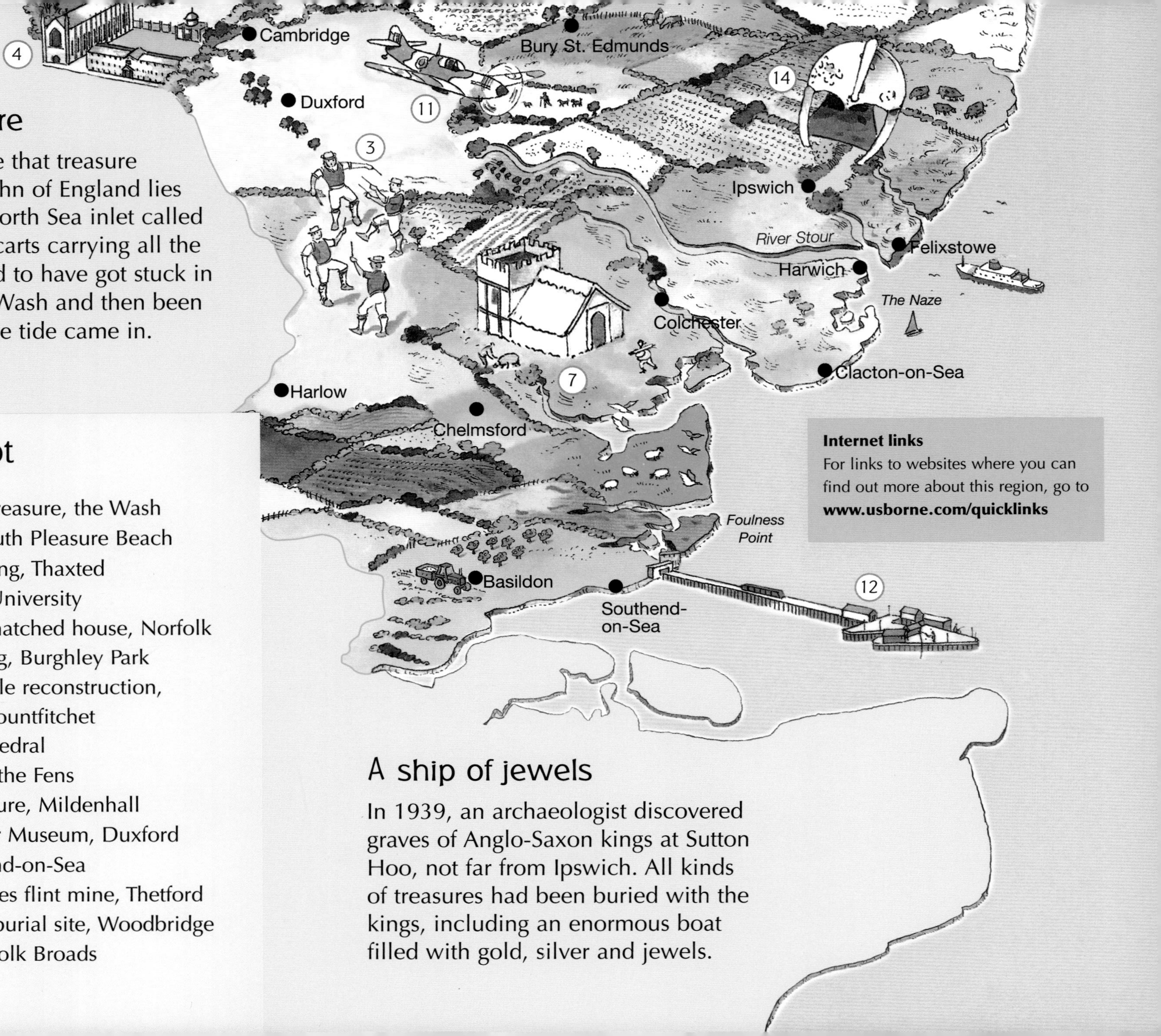
4
Cambridge
Duxford
11
Bury St. Edmunds
14
3
Ipswich
River Stour
Felixstowe
Harwich
The Naze
Colchester
Clacton-on-Sea
7
Harlow
Chelmsford
Foulness
Point
Basildon
Southend-
on-Sea
12

Sunken treasure

Some people believe that treasure belonging to King John of England lies at the bottom of a North Sea inlet called the Wash. In 1216, carts carrying all the king's jewels are said to have got stuck in quicksand near the Wash and then been swept away when the tide came in.

Things to spot

1 King John's treasure, the Wash
2 Great Yarmouth Pleasure Beach
3 Morris dancing, Thaxted
4 Cambridge University
5 Traditional thatched house, Norfolk
6 Showjumping, Burghley Park
7 Norman castle reconstruction, Stansted Mountfitchet
8 Lincoln Cathedral
9 Windpump, the Fens
10 Roman treasure, Mildenhall
11 Imperial War Museum, Duxford
12 Pier, Southend-on-Sea
13 Grimes Graves flint mine, Thetford
14 Sutton Hoo burial site, Woodbridge
15 Sailing, Norfolk Broads

Internet links
For links to websites where you can find out more about this region, go to **www.usborne.com/quicklinks**

A ship of jewels

In 1939, an archaeologist discovered graves of Anglo-Saxon kings at Sutton Hoo, not far from Ipswich. All kinds of treasures had been buried with the kings, including an enormous boat filled with gold, silver and jewels.

The West Midlands

Internet links

For links to websites where you can find out more about this region, go to **www.usborne.com/quicklinks**

The Midlands make up central England, and the western part extends to the Welsh border. The area has a long history of making pottery, china, chocolate and many other products.

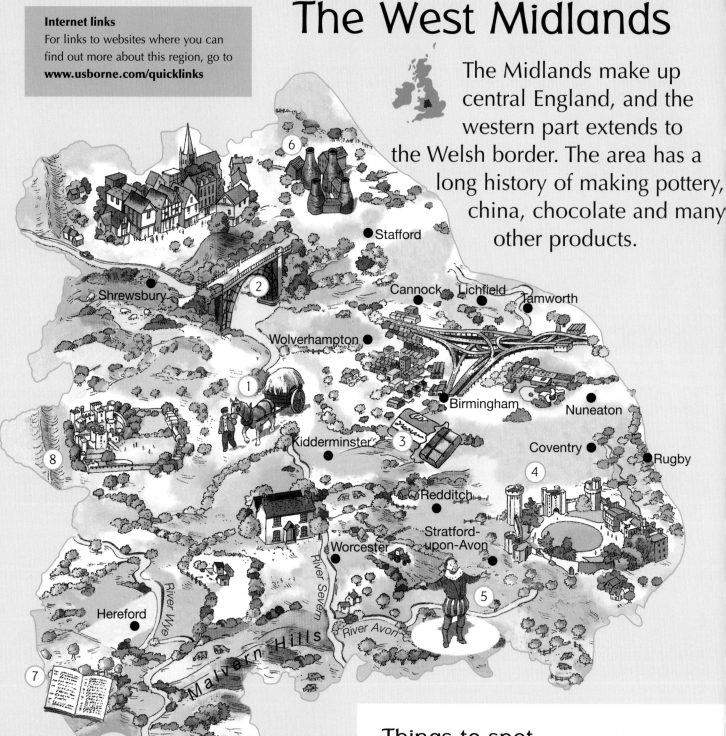

Stafford

Shrewsbury

Cannock Lichfield Tamworth

Wolverhampton

Birmingham Nuneaton

Kidderminster Coventry Rugby

Redditch

Stratford-upon-Avon

Worcester

Hereford

River Wye

River Severn

River Avon

Malvern Hills

Shakespeare's home

The playwright William Shakespeare was born in the town of Stratford-upon-Avon in 1564. Thousands of visitors flock there every year to see the house where he was born, and to watch performances of his plays by the Royal Shakespeare Company.

Things to spot

1 Acton Scott Historic Working Farm
2 Iron Bridge, Telford
3 Cadbury World, Bournville
4 Warwick Castle
5 Shakespearean play, Stratford-upon-Avon
6 Pottery factories
7 Book shops, Hay-on-Wye
8 Ludlow Castle

The East Midlands

The East Midlands have lots of scenic countryside, including the Peak District and Sherwood Forest.

Robin Hood

Robin Hood was a legendary outlaw and hero who is said to have lived in Sherwood Forest in the Middle Ages. Many stories are told of his daring adventures.

Deer dance

The village of Abbots Bromley has an annual event called the Horn Dance. It dates back to the thirteenth century and involves local men performing dances while carrying deer antlers.

Things to spot

1. Alton Towers theme park
2. Robin Hood exhibition, Sherwood Forest
3. Butterfly and Aquatic Centre, Oakham
4. Heights of Abraham, Matlock Bath
5. Horn Dance, Abbots Bromley
6. Balloon festival, Northampton
7. Donington Park racetrack
8. Castleton Caverns

Internet links
For links to websites where you can find out more about this region, go to **www.usborne.com/quicklinks**

Northwest England

In the far northwest of England is the Lake District, a huge national park that contains beautiful lakes and mountains and is a popular place for walking, sailing and climbing trips. Further south are the busy cities of Liverpool and Manchester.

Beatrix Potter

Beatrix Potter wrote and illustrated famous stories about Peter Rabbit and other characters. She was born in 1866 in London, but she loved the Lake District and spent most of her time there.

Internet links

For links to websites where you can find out more about this region, go to **www.usborne.com/quicklinks**

Pennines

Carlisle

Penrith

8

10

14

Keswick

Scafell Pike

Lake District

Kendal

1

Solway Firth

Workington

Whitehaven

St. Bees Head

12

Isle of Man

9

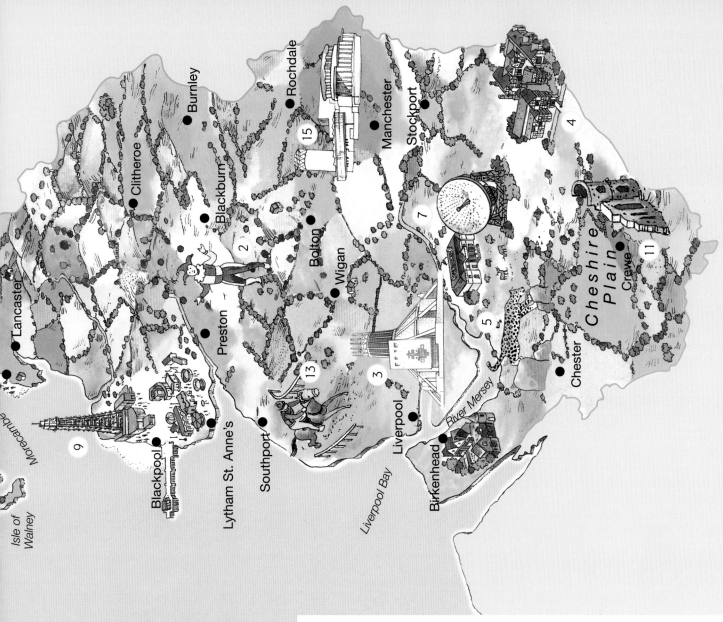

Blackpool

Blackpool is one of Britain's busiest seaside resorts. It has a zoo, three piers, funfair rides and many other kinds of amusements. Its most famous building is Blackpool Tower, which was modelled on the Eiffel Tower, in Paris. It contains a ballroom, an aquarium and a circus.

IRISH SEA

Isle of Walney

Morecambe

Lancaster

Clitheroe

Burnley

Blackburn

Rochdale

Manchester

Stockport

Bolton

Wigan

Preston

Lytham St. Anne's

Southport

Liverpool

Liverpool Bay

Birkenhead

River Mersey

Chester

Crewe

Cheshire Plain

Blackpool

Things to spot

1   Lake Windermere
2   Camelot theme park, Chorley
3   Liverpool Metropolitan Cathedral
4   Little Moreton Hall, Congleton
5   Chester Zoo
6   Lady Isabella waterwheel
7   Lovell Telescope, Jodrell Bank
8   Hang-gliding, Lake District
9   Blackpool Tower
10 Cumberland and Westmoreland wrestling
11 Mow Cop Castle
12 Beatrix Potter's home
13 Horseracing, Aintree racecourse
14 Cumberland Pencil Museum, Keswick
15 The Lowry, Salford

Northeast England

Northeast England has huge areas of rugged, windswept countryside. There are also many picturesque cities, including Durham and York.

Things to spot

1. Trams, Beamish Open Air Museum
2. Lightwater Valley theme park
3. The Deep, Kingston upon Hull
4. Medieval fair, Alnwick
5. Ski Village, Sheffield
6. Holy Island (Lindisfarne)
7. York Minster
8. Angel of the North, Gateshead
9. National Museum of Photography, Film and Television, Bradford
10. Kielder Water
11. North Yorkshire Moors Railway
12. Cheese-making, Wensleydale
13. Humber Bridge
14. Hadrian's Wall
15. The Locomotion, Darlington Railway Museum
16. Jousting re-enactment, Royal Armouries Museum, Leeds

Internet links

For links to websites where you can find out more about this region, go to
www.usborne.com/quicklinks

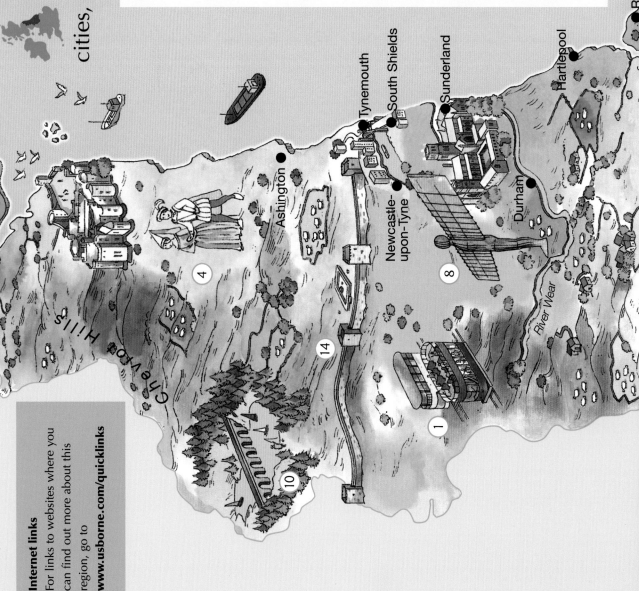

Berwick-upon-Tweed

Cheviot Hills

Ashington

Tynemouth

South Shields

Newcastle-upon-Tyne

Sunderland

Durham

River Wear

Hartlepool

Redcar

NORTH SEA

Robin Hood's Bay

Whitby

Scarborough

Flamborough Head

Bridlington Bay

Bridlington

Yorkshire Wolds

Kingston upon Hull

Grimsby

Scunthorpe

River Ouse

York

Pennines

Ripon

Skipton

Harrogate

Leeds

Bradford

Huddersfield

Barnsley

Doncaster

Rotherham

Sheffield

Roman wall

About 2,000 years ago, much of Britain was ruled by the Romans. Emperor Hadrian ordered the building of a wall to mark the northern border of their land and to keep out tribes from further north. Parts of the wall still stand.

Medieval glass

York Minster is a magnificent cathedral that was built in the Middle Ages. It has 128 stained glass windows, and the East Window is the largest piece of medieval stained glass in the world.

Sharks at The Deep

The Deep is a high-tech aquarium where visitors can take an underwater elevator through a gigantic tank and see sharks, rays, eels and other amazing creatures up close.

Wales

Wales is a country of high mountains and deep valleys. Its capital is Cardiff, in the southeast. In the Middle Ages, Wales was often invaded by the English, and many big stone castles were built there.

Welsh festivals

Wales has a yearly folk festival called the Eisteddfod, which means "gathering" in Welsh. It is a week-long celebration of Welsh culture, and is held in a different place each year. There is also a musical Eisteddfod in Llangollen every July, where competitors from around the world take part in music, dance and song contests.

Going underground

Coal mining was once a vital industry in Wales. The Big Pit mine in Blaenafon shut in 1980 and is now a mining museum. Visitors go 90m (300ft) underground to learn what life was like for the many miners who used to dig for coal there.

Liverpool Bay

Flint

Rhyl

Great Ormes Head · Llandudno

Anglesey

Holyhead

Holy Island

Bangor

Caernarfon Bay

Menai Strait

Porthmadog

Pwllheli

Tremadog Bay

Braich y Pwll

Bardsey Island

Blaenau Ffestiniog

Dolgellau

Cardigan Bay

Aberystwyth

Aberaeron

Welshpool

Newtown

Radnor Forest

Cambrian Mountains

2 · 7 · 5 · 9 · 6 · 13 · 3 · 10 · 8

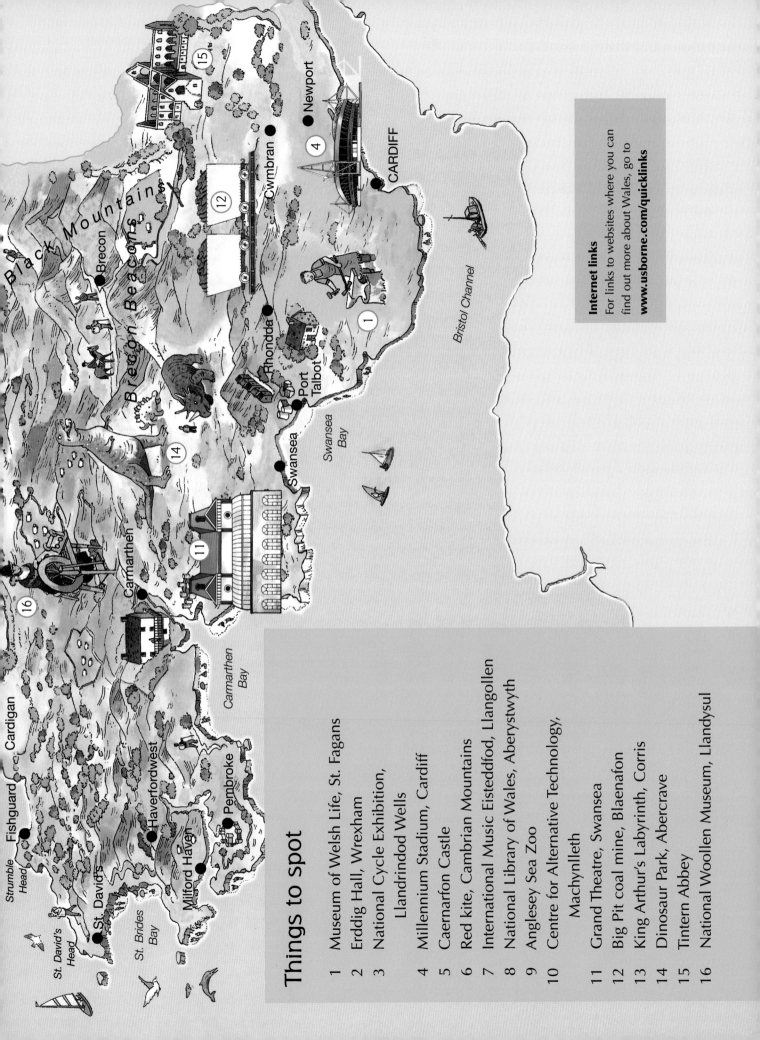

Things to spot

1 Museum of Welsh Life, St. Fagans
2 Erddig Hall, Wrexham
3 National Cycle Exhibition, Llandrindod Wells
4 Millennium Stadium, Cardiff
5 Caernarfon Castle
6 Red kite, Cambrian Mountains
7 International Music Eisteddfod, Llangollen
8 National Library of Wales, Aberystwyth
9 Anglesey Sea Zoo
10 Centre for Alternative Technology, Machynlleth
11 Grand Theatre, Swansea
12 Big Pit coal mine, Blaenafon
13 King Arthur's Labyrinth, Corris
14 Dinosaur Park, Abercrave
15 Tintern Abbey
16 National Woollen Museum, Llandysul

Southern Scotland

Southern Scotland is known as the Lowlands, because it has fewer mountains than northern Scotland. Scotland's capital city, Edinburgh, is in the south, as is the country's biggest city, Glasgow.

A royal castle

Edinburgh Castle stands on an enormous rock, high above the city. The castle was the home of Scottish kings and is made up of many buildings, including a 12th-century chapel.

Internet links
For links to websites where you can find out more about this region, go to www.usborne.com/quicklinks

St. Abb's Head

North Berwick

Firth of Forth

Lammermuir Hills

EDINBURGH

Pentland Hills

Peebles

Greenock

River Clyde

Paisley

Glasgow

Hamilton

River Clyde

Kilmarnock

Irvine

Firth of Clyde

Things to spot

1. Dolphins, Solway Firth
2. Forth Rail Bridge
3. Museum of Lead Mining, Wanlockhead
4. Glasgow Science Centre
5. Caerlaverock Castle
6. Edinburgh Castle
7. Melrose Abbey
8. Falkirk Wheel boat lift
9. Vikingar exhibition, Largs
10. Robert Burns statue, Dumfries
11. Wool mill, Galashiels
12. Fishing, Solway Firth
13. Blowplain Farm, Balmaclellan
14. Common Riding Festival, Selkirk
15. Mountain biking, Southern Uplands

Robert Burns

Scotland's best-known poet is Robert Burns. He was born in Alloway on 25 January 1759, and later lived in Dumfries. His birthday is remembered every year with a celebration called Burns Night.

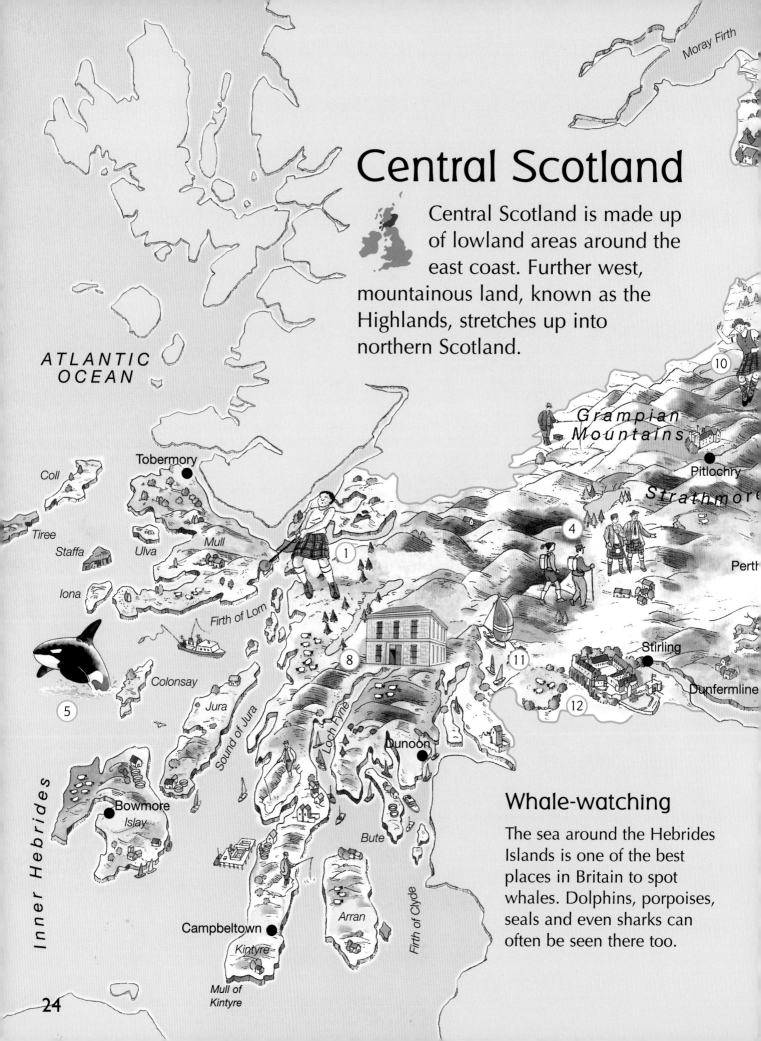

Central Scotland

Central Scotland is made up of lowland areas around the east coast. Further west, mountainous land, known as the Highlands, stretches up into northern Scotland.

ATLANTIC OCEAN

Moray Firth

Grampian Mountains

Pitlochry

Strathmore

Perth

Stirling

Dunfermline

Tobermory

Coll

Tiree

Staffa

Ulva

Mull

Iona

Firth of Lorn

Colonsay

Jura

Sound of Jura

Loch Fyne

Dunoon

Inner Hebrides

Bowmore

Islay

Bute

Firth of Clyde

Campbeltown

Kintyre

Arran

Mull of Kintyre

Whale-watching

The sea around the Hebrides Islands is one of the best places in Britain to spot whales. Dolphins, porpoises, seals and even sharks can often be seen there too.

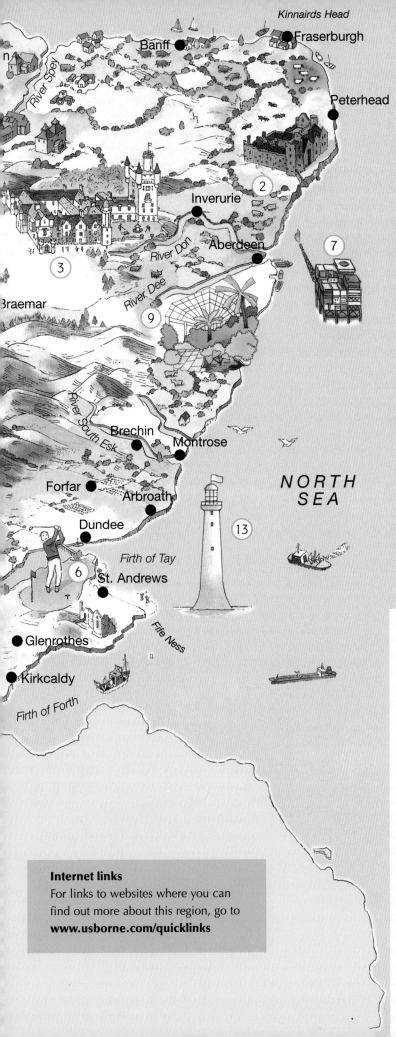

Traditional sports

The Highland Games are displays of traditional Scottish sports, dance and music, and are held in towns throughout Scotland every summer. Events such as throwing heavy weights or tossing the caber, a huge, trimmed tree trunk, require a lot of strength.

Creepy castle

Slains Castle stands on a jagged cliff edge on the North Sea coast. It was built in 1597 and is now in ruins. The author Bram Stoker visited the castle in 1895, and might have used it in his novel *Dracula* as the model for Dracula's spooky home.

Things to spot

1 Throwing the weight, Highland Games, Oban
2 Slains Castle, Cruden Bay
3 Balmoral Castle
4 Walking, the Trossachs
5 Killer whale, Hebrides
6 Golfing, St. Andrews
7 Oil platform, North Sea
8 Inveraray Jail
9 Duthie Park Winter Gardens, Aberdeen
10 Highland dancing
11 Loch Lomond
12 Stirling Castle
13 Bell Rock Lighthouse

Internet links
For links to websites where you can find out more about this region, go to
www.usborne.com/quicklinks

Northern Scotland

Northern Scotland is one of the most unspoilt parts of Britain. Its stunning Highland scenery includes mountains, moors and lochs, which are lakes or long sea inlets.

ATLANTIC OCEAN

Outer Hebrides

Butt of Lewis

Cape Wrath

Eddrachillis Bay

2

9

Lewis

Harris

The Minch

Gruinard Bay

Stornoway

Ullapool

3

Loch Torridon

North Uist

Benbecula

South Uist

Inner Hebrides

Skye

Portree

Cuillin Hills

Kyle of Lochalsh

14

Barra

Loch monster

There are many stories about a giant, humpbacked monster that is said to live in Loch Ness. Some people claim to have caught glimpses of a strange creature there, but nothing has ever been proved.

7

Rhum (Rum)

Eigg

Point of Ardnamurchan

Sound of Sleat

Mallaig

Glen

13

Ben Ne

Fort William

Loch Linnhe

Northern islands

The Orkney Islands are a group of scenic islands just off the northeast tip of mainland Scotland. Further north still are the rugged, windswept Shetland Islands, the most northerly part of Britain.

High ride

Britain's highest mountain, Ben Nevis, is 1,343m (4,406ft) high. You can get good views of it by taking a cable car up a nearby mountain called Aonach Mòr.

Things to spot

1 Highland Wildlife Park, Kincraig
2 Calanais Standing Stones, Lewis
3 Golden eagle, Beinn Eighe nature reserve
4 Diving for wrecks, Pentland Firth
5 Panning for gold, Baile an Or
6 Ski resort, Aviemore
7 Skye Serpentarium, Broadford
8 Cable car, Aonach Mòr
9 Harris tweed worker
10 Sea otters, Kyle of Tongue
11 Cawdor Castle
12 Loch Ness monster
13 Glenfinnan Viaduct
14 Historical weapons show, Clansman Centre, Fort Augustus
15 Puffins, Dornoch Firth

Internet links
For links to websites where you can find out more about this region, go to
www.usborne.com/quicklinks

Map labels

Orkney Islands

To the Shetland Islands

Pentland Firth

John o' Groats

Thurso

Wick

Helmsdale

NORTH SEA

Tarbat Ness

Invergordon

Cromarty Firth

Moray Firth

Dingwall

Inverness

10
4
5
15
11
12
1
6

Northern Ireland

Northern Ireland's varied landscape includes mountains, farmland and lakes called loughs. Its capital is Belfast, a large city which is home to around a sixth of the country's population.

Internet links
For links to websites where you can find out more about this region, go to
www.usborne.com/quicklinks

Ireland's saint

On March 17th, Irish people celebrate St. Patrick's Day. St. Patrick was a famous fifth-century bishop who is buried in Downpatrick.

Belfast cranes

Samson and Goliath are two towering cranes that belong to a shipbuilding company. They dominate the Belfast skyline and are well-known symbols of Belfast's long history of shipbuilding.

Things to spot

1 Samson and Goliath cranes, Belfast
2 Tenth century stone cross, Ardboe
3 Giant's Causeway
4 Devenish Monastery
5 Peatlands Country Park, Dungannon
6 Ulster Folk and Transport Museum
7 St. Patrick's Day parade, Downpatrick
8 Dunluce Castle
9 Ulster History Park
10 Marble Arch Caves
11 Spanish Armada treasure,
       Ulster Museum, Belfast
12 Navan Fort, Armagh
13 Hurling game, Maghera
14 Medieval city walls, Londonderry
15 Dodo Terrace, Mount Stewart House,
       Newtownards
16 Ulster American Folk Park, Omagh

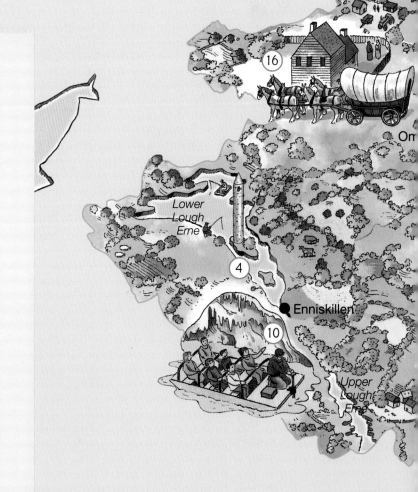

Londonderry (Derry)

Strab

Om

Lower Lough Erne

Enniskillen

Upper Lough Erne

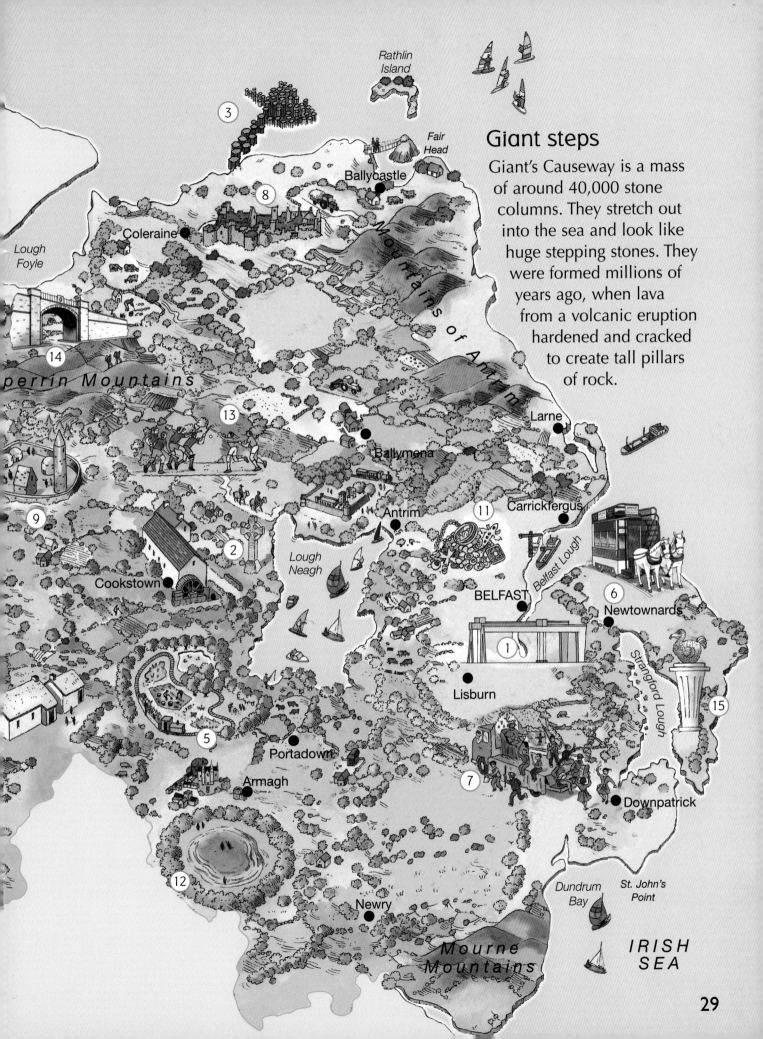

Giant steps

Giant's Causeway is a mass of around 40,000 stone columns. They stretch out into the sea and look like huge stepping stones. They were formed millions of years ago, when lava from a volcanic eruption hardened and cracked to create tall pillars of rock.

Rathlin Island

Fair Head

Ballycastle

Coleraine

Lough Foyle

perrin Mountains

Mountains of Antrim

Larne

Ballymena

Antrim

Carrickfergus

Lough Neagh

Belfast Lough

BELFAST

Newtownards

Cookstown

Lisburn

Strangford Lough

Portadown

Armagh

Downpatrick

Newry

Dundrum Bay

St. John's Point

Mourne Mountains

IRISH SEA

Index

Acton Scott Historic Working Farm, 14

Alton Towers theme park, 15

Angel of the North, Gateshead, 18

Anglesey Sea Zoo, 20

Balloon festival, Northampton, 15

Balmoral Castle, 25

Beatrix Potter's home, 16

Bedruthan Steps, 6

Bekonscot Model Village, Beaconsfield, 11

Bell Rock Lighthouse, 25

Big Pit coal mine, Blaenafon, 21

Blackpool Tower, 17

Blowplain Farm, Balmaclellan, 23

Bluebell Railway, near East Grinstead, 9

Boating, Hyde Park, 4

Book shops, Hay-on-Wye, 14

British Museum, 4

Butterfly and Aquatic Centre, Oakham, 15

Cable car, Aonach Mòr, 26

Cadbury World, Bournville, 14

Caerlaverock Castle, 23

Caernarfon Castle, 20

Calanais Standing Stones, Lewis, 26

Cambridge University, 12

Camelot theme park, Chorley, 17

Canterbury Cathedral, 9

Castleton Caverns, 15

Cawdor Castle, 27

Centre for Alternative Technology,
  Machynlleth, 20

Channel Tunnel, 9

Cheese-making, Wensleydale, 19

Chessington World of Adventures, 8

Chester Zoo, 17

Chinese New Year parade, 4

Clifton Suspension Bridge, Bristol, 10

Clock tower, Houses of Parliament, 5

Common Riding Festival, Selkirk, 23

Cotswold Farm Park, Stow-on-the-Wold, 10

Cricket match, Hambledon, 8

Cumberland and Westmoreland wrestling, 16

Cumberland Pencil Museum, Keswick, 16

Deep, the, Kingston upon Hull, 19

Deer, Exmoor National Park, 7

Devenish Monastery, 28

Dinosaur, Natural History Museum, 4

Dinosaur Park, Abercrave, 21

Diving for wrecks, Pentland Firth, 27

Dodo Terrace, Mount Stewart House,
  Newtownards, 29

Dolphins, Solway Firth, 23

Donington Park racetrack, 15

Dover Castle, 9

Drusillas Park, Alfriston, 9

Dunluce Castle, 29

Duthie Park Winter Gardens, Aberdeen, 25

Eden Project, 6

Edinburgh Castle, 22

Erddig Hall, Wrexham, 20

Exeter Cathedral, 7

Falkirk Wheel boat lift, 22

Farnborough International air show, 8

Fishing, Solway Firth, 23

Forth Rail Bridge, 22

Gatwick Airport, 9

Georgian houses, Bath, 10

Giant's Causeway, 29

Glasgow Science Centre, 22

Glastonbury Abbey, 7

Glenfinnan Viaduct, 26

Golden eagle, Beinn Eighe nature
  reserve, 26

Golfing, St. Andrews, 25

Grand Theatre, Swansea, 21

Great Yarmouth Pleasure Beach, 12

Grimes Graves flint mine, Thetford, 12

Guard, Buckingham Palace, 4

Hadrian's Wall, 18

Hamleys toy store, 4

Hang-gliding, Lake District, 16

Harris tweed worker, 26

Hatfield House, 11

Heights of Abraham, Matlock Bath, 15

Highland dancing, 24

Highland Wildlife Park, Kincraig, 27

Historical weapons show, Clansman
  Centre, Fort Augustus, 26

HMS Belfast, 5

HMS Victory, Portsmouth, 8

Holy Island (Lindisfarne), 18

Horn Dance, Abbots Bromley, 15

Horseracing, Aintree racecourse, 17

Humber Bridge, 19

Hurling game, Maghera, 29

Imperial War Museum, Duxford, 13

International Music Eisteddfod, Llangollen, 20

Inveraray Jail, 24

Iron Bridge, Telford, 14

Jousting re-enactment, Royal
  Armouries Museum, Leeds, 19

Kielder Water, 18

Killer whale, Hebrides Sea, 24

King Arthur exhibition, Corris, 20

King John's treasure, the Wash, 12

Lady Isabella waterwheel, 16

Lake Windermere, 16

Leeds Castle, 9

Lightwater Valley theme park, 19

Lincoln Cathedral, 12

Little Moreton Hall, Congleton, 17

Liverpool Metropolitan Cathedral, 17

Loch Lomond, 24

Loch Ness monster, 26

Locomotion, the, Darlington Railway Museum, 19

London bus, 4

London Eye, 5

Lovell Telescope, Jodrell Bank, 17

Lowry, the, Salford, 17

Ludlow Castle, 14

Maiden Castle hill fort, Dorchester, 8

Marble Arch Caves, 28

Maypole dancing, Ickwell Green, 11

Maze, Longleat House, Warminster, 10

Medieval city walls, Londonderry, 28

Medieval fair, Alnwick, 18

Melrose Abbey, 22

Millennium Stadium, Cardiff, 21

Morris dancing, Thaxted, 13

Mountain biking, Southern Uplands, 22

Mow Cop Castle, 17

Museum of Lead Mining, Wanlockhead, 23

Museum of Welsh Life, St. Fagans, 21

National Cycle Exhibition, Llandrindod Wells, 20

National Library of Wales, Aberystwyth, 20

National Motor Museum, Beaulieu, 8

National Museum of Photography, Film
  and Television, Bradford, 19

National Woollen Museum, Llandysul, 21

Navan Fort, Armagh, 29

Nelson's Column, 4

Norman castle reconstruction, Stansted
  Mountfitchet, 13

North Yorkshire Moors Railway, 19

Oil platform, North Sea, 25

Olympic Stadium, London, 9

Ottery St. Mary fire festival, 7

Panning for gold, Baile an Or, 27

Parrot, London Zoo, 4

Peatlands Country Park, Dungannon, 29

Pier, Southend-on-Sea, 13

Poldark Tin Mine, 6

Ponies, Dartmoor, 7

Pottery factories, 14

Puffins, Dornoch Firth, 27

Red kite, Cambrian Mountains, 20

Robert Burns statue, Dumfries, 23

Robin Hood exhibition, Sherwood Forest, 15

Royal Pavilion, Brighton, 9

Sailing, Norfolk Broads, 12

St. Michael's Mount, 6

St. Patrick's Day parade, Downpatrick, 29
St. Paul's Cathedral, 5
Samson and Goliath cranes, Belfast, 29
Sculpture Trail, Forest of Dean, 10
Sea otters, Kyle of Tongue, 27
Shakespearean play, Stratford-upon-Avon, 14
Shakespeare's Globe, 5
Showjumping, Burghley Park, 12
Ski resort, Aviemore, 27
Ski Village, Sheffield, 19
Skye Serpentarium, Broadford, 26
Slains Castle, Cruden Bay, 25
Somerset apples, 7
Spanish Armada treasure, Ulster Museum,
 Belfast, 29
Stirling Castle, 24
Stone circle, Avebury, 10
Stonehenge, 10
Student, Oxford University, 11
Surfing, Atlantic Ocean, 6
Sutton Hoo burial site, Woodbridge, 13
Tenth century stone cross, Ardboe, 29
Throwing the weight, Highland Games, Oban, 24

Tintagel Castle, 6
Tintern Abbey, 21
Torquay beach, 7
Tower Bridge, 5
Tower of London, 5
Traditional thatched house, Norfolk, 12
Trams, Beamish Open Air Museum, 18
Treasure, Mildenhall, 12
Tropical garden, Tresco, 6
Ulster American Folk Park, Omagh, 28
Ulster Folk and Transport Museum, 29
Ulster History Park, 28
Vikingar exhibition, Largs, 22
Walking, the Trossachs, 24
Warwick Castle, 14
Whipsnade Wild Animal Park, Dunstable, 11
White Horse, Uffington, 10
Wildfowl and Wetlands Centre, Slimbridge, 10
Windpump, the Fens, 12
Windsor Castle, 11
Wookey Hole Caves, 7
Wool mill, Galashiels, 22
Yachting, near the Isle of Wight, 8

Edited by Gillian Doherty and Louie Stowell
Cartographic editor: Craig Asquith
Consultants: Dr. Gillian McIntosh, Queen's University Belfast;
Dr. James Oliver, University of Edinburgh;
Dr. Paul Readman, King's College London;
Dr. Steven Thompson, University of Wales, Aberystwyth
With thanks to Fiona Patchett and Alice Pearcey
Cover design by Stephen Moncrieff and Sam Chandler
Digital manipulation by Katie Mayes, Mike Olley
and Nick Wakeford